THE STORY OF

LOUISA MAY ALCOTT, Determined Writer

BY MARCI RIDLON MCGILL

ILLUSTRATED BY DARCY MAY

A YEARLING BOOK

ABOUT THIS BOOK

The events described in this book are true. They have been carefully researched and excerpted from authentic autobiographies, writings, and commentaries. No part of this biography has been fictionalized.

To learn more about Louisa May Alcott, ask your librarian to recommend other fine books you might read.

Published by
Dell Publishing
a division of
Bantam Doubleday Dell Publishing Group, Inc.
666 Fifth Avenue
New York, New York 10103

ISBN: 0-440-40022-8

Published by arrangement with Parachute Press, Inc.
Printed in the United States of America
April 1988

10 9 8 7 6 5 4 3

CW

Contents

New Beginnings   1

On the Go   6

"Now the flowers blossom gay"   12

Working Together   19

A Room of Her Own   31

Helping Out   39

Changes in the Wind   47

Nurse Louisa   62

"A Girls' Book"   73

A Job Well Done   83

Highlights in the Life of Louisa May
    Alcott   90

Works by Louisa May Alcott   92

New Beginnings

THE COLD MARCH WIND RATTLED THE windows of the rambling brown house, but that didn't bother thirteen-year-old Louisa May Alcott. She was snug and cozy in the first room of her own that she had ever had. Even though Louisa loved her family more than anything else in the world, she also loved to be alone with her own thoughts and ideas. Her desk was by the window, so that she could look out at the garden from time to time as she wrote in her journal or worked on stories or plays.

Young Louisa was pleased whenever her family and friends praised her writing. But she had no idea that she would grow up to be a famous writer whose best-known book, *Little Women,* would be read and enjoyed by millions of readers.

Louisa May Alcott was born in German-town, Pennsylvania, on November 29, 1832, to Bronson and Abigail May (known as Abba) Alcott. Bronson and Abba Alcott came from very different backgrounds. Bronson's parents were poor farmers. His mother could not read or write very well, because she had not been given an education. In those days only boys whose families could afford to send them went to school. Girls usually were expected to stay home and learn housekeeping. But Bronson's mother valued education, kept a journal, and encouraged Bronson to study and learn at home. Because of this she was a very big influence in his life.

Bronson's wife, Abba, was a member of the well-to-do May family of Boston. Her aunt had been married to John Hancock, the first governor of Massachusetts and one of the signers of the Declaration of Independence. Other members of her family were important in politics, the law, education, and the church.

Louisa's parents were different in ways other than family background. Bronson was tall, blond, and blue-eyed. He was a gentle dreamer and a man of ideas. Abba had dark hair and eyes and was a practical woman of action who often had difficulty controlling her fiery temper, but she was also very generous and warm.

The Alcotts had come from New England to Pennsylvania in 1831, the year before Louisa's birth, at the request of Reuben Haines, an important member of the Quaker community in Germantown. Mr. Haines wanted to start a number of schools in his town and pay for them himself. He had been impressed with Bronson Alcott, who was becoming known as a man with very different ideas about teaching.

Unlike many people of his day, Bronson believed that girls as well as boys should be allowed to go to school. Bronson also listened carefully to what children had to say. He asked their opinions and treated them with respect at a time when most other adults thought children "should be seen and not heard." Bronson did all he could to make his lessons lively and interesting, since he felt that that was the way children learned best. Reuben Haines agreed with his ideas, and the two men became dear friends.

Mr. Haines provided a rent-free house, known as Pine Place, for the Alcotts to live in and to use for the school. It was a square farmhouse surrounded by pine trees, with streams and rivers nearby. There was also a lovely walk on the grounds which was shaded by plum, pear, peach, fir, apple, and cedar trees.

Louisa May was the Alcotts' second daughter. Their first daughter, Anna, also known as Nan, was born March 16, 1831, shortly after the Alcotts arrived in Germantown. Although the two girls were only a year and a half apart they were very different. Anna was a quiet, contented baby most of the time, but Louisa was very lively right from the start. She would jump and wiggle in her mother's arms, always eager to get down and be on her own, always interested in exploring whatever was new or different.

The Alcotts were very happy at Pine Place, and they would have liked to have stayed there. They had a lovely house, servants, and the beautiful countryside in which to roam. But not long after they settled in, Reuben Haines died. He had provided money, direction, and support for Bronson's new ways of teaching. Although Bronson was able to continue the school for two years, it was not the same. The parents of his students began to doubt his methods and to take their children out of school. There were fewer and fewer students, and so Pine Place was closed in April of 1833.

The Alcotts moved to Philadelphia, and Bronson started another school. But again people did not understand his new methods of education, and parents gradually withdrew their children. The Alcotts decided to return to Boston. Bronson felt that he would be able to get the necessary money and support in Boston to start another school, which he hoped would be more successful.

The Alcotts were sad to leave their many good friends in Pennsylvania, but they were hopeful that things would be better for them where they were going. So in 1834, at the age of two, little Louisa was about to make the second major move of her young life.

On the Go

LOUISA AND HER SISTER ANNA WERE ALL dressed up for the trip. On a steamer headed for Boston, the family excitedly talked about the new life that was about to begin.

Soon after they arrived in the busy seaport city, Bronson opened a new school called the Temple School, which was quite famous for a while. It started with thirty students who were from some of Boston's best families. Bronson's assistant was Miss Elizabeth Peabody, who later did a great deal to start kindergarten teaching in America. But at this time she was still learning herself, and she learned a lot from Bronson Alcott.

While the Alcotts lived in Boston, two more babies were born to the family. The first was Elizabeth, named after Elizabeth Peabody, in 1835. (Elizabeth was also called Lizzie, Beth, or Betty.) Then a little boy was born, but he did not live very long. This was a very sad time for the whole family, but they carried on in spite of their grief.

Some of Louisa May Alcott's earliest memories were of this time in Boston. She remembered especially her fourth birthday, which was celebrated at her father's Temple School with all the children present. Louisa wore a crown of flowers and stood on a table to give each child a plum cake. But someone had made a mistake, and there were not enough cakes to go around. Lousia saw that if she gave away the last one, there would be none for her. She felt that since it was her birthday and she was queen of the party, she should be the one to have it. Louisa held on to it tightly until her mother said, "It is always better to give away than to keep the nice things; so I know my Louy will not let the little friend go without."

Louisa gave her friend the cake and received a kiss from her mother and what she believed was an important lesson: think of others before oneself.

Another of Louisa's earliest memories was

of playing with books in her father's study— building houses and bridges of the big dictionaries and diaries, looking at pictures, pretending to read, and scribbling on blank pages with pen or pencil.

On one occasion she and Anna built a high tower around their baby sister Lizzie as she sat playing with her toys on the floor. Then something attracted the older girls' attention out-of-doors, and they forgot all about their little captive. When later the baby was missing, a search was made, and she was found where she had been left— curled up fast asleep, enclosed in her book-tower walls. But Lizzie awoke so rested and happy from her nap that Anna and Louisa were forgiven for having forgotten about their little sister.

As an adult Louisa wrote: "Running away was one of the delights of my early days; and I still enjoy sudden flights out of the nest to look about this very interesting world, and then go back to report."

Louisa remembered one day in particular when she wandered off to see something of Boston by herself when her mother wasn't looking. She went from street to street, playing with some Irish children who "shared their cold potatoes, salt-fish, and crusts with me. . . ." As it began to get dark, her friends left her, and she "felt that home was a nice place after all, and tried to find it."

She stopped to rest on some doorsteps and, while watching a lamplighter, fell asleep with her head on the curly back of a big friendly dog. Louisa was awakened by the sound of the town crier's bell. He had been sent in search of her by her frantic parents. He called out: "Lost, a little girl, six years old, in a pink frock, white hat, and new green shoes!"

First Louisa wondered who he could be talking about, but then in a flash she knew. "Why, dat's me!" she called back.

The town crier carried her to his house, where she enjoyed eating bread and molasses in a tin plate bordered with alphabet letters. Her worried parents came for her as quickly as they could and there were lots of hugs and kisses. But the next day she had to stay on the sofa as a punishment for her adventure.

Louisa's sister Anna was old enough to go to her father's school, but Louisa was not.

She often spent mornings with her mother on the Common, a large grassy place near their house on Front Street. The Common was her favorite place, because there was so much to see and do. There were always dogs, cats, and other children romping on the grass. And she loved the Frog Pond, where she could sit and toss small stones into the water and watch the ripples.

Louisa's mother always watched her carefully, but one day, when her mother's back was turned for just a moment, Louisa got too close to the edge of the pond and fell in. The water was cold and deep, way over Louisa's head. She was very afraid as she splashed and splashed, fighting to stay on top. The grown-ups around her did not know what to do.

A young black boy knew what to do, though. He rushed over to the pond, jumped in, and pulled Louisa to safety. Then he smiled at her and slipped away before anyone could thank him or ask his name. Louisa remembered what had happened that day for the rest of her life—the gasping and sinking, and then the strong arms and friendly face of the boy who had saved her.

"Now the flowers blossom gay"

ALTHOUGH THE CIVIL WAR WOULD NOT begin until 1861, people were talking a lot about slavery. The country was already divided between those who thought slavery should be allowed and those who thought it was very wrong and should be done away with. Bronson and Abba Alcott were among those who wanted to do away with slavery.

Louisa was only seven, but she also understood that slavery was wrong. She had heard how her father's good friend William Lloyd Garrison was almost hanged by a mob because of his speeches saying that the slaves should be set free. And she had not forgotten the young black boy who had pulled her out of the Frog Pond.

Louisa did not realize that being against slavery would affect her family in an important way. Bronson had let a little black girl come to his school because he believed so strongly that black children also had a right to an education. He wanted his school to be open to everyone, but the parents of his students did not agree. Gradually they withdrew their children from Temple School, and it had to close. Bronson paid many times for his beliefs, but he stuck to them and did not give up.

Ralph Waldo Emerson, a famous writer and thinker who was a very good friend of the Alcotts, told Bronson that they would like Concord, Massachusetts, where he lived. It didn't take long for the family to decide to move to Concord. Moving was never difficult for the Alcotts, and they were almost always excited about it. A good thing, too, since they moved twenty-nine times during the first twenty-eight years of Louisa's life!

The house the Alcotts went to in Concord was called the Hosmer Cottage, and it turned out to be a place of great happiness for Louisa. There was much more room to roam than there had been in Boston. The house had a big garden with fields filled with daisies and mayflowers. A river ran through the meadow nearby. There were also beautiful hills covered with pink mountain laurel and pine woods within easy reach.

Louisa loved to be outdoors, free to run through the fields or watch the birds in the garden. Running was an important part of her life. She once wrote, "I always thought I must have been a deer or a horse in some former state, because it was such a joy to run."

It was at this time that Louisa began to write. When she was eight years old, she wrote this poem called "To the First Robin."

Welcome, welcome, little stranger,
Fear no harm, and fear no danger;
We are glad to see you here,
For you sing, "Sweet Spring is near."

Now the white snow melts away;
Now the flowers blossom gay:
Come dear bird and build your nest,
For we love our robin best.

Louisa enjoyed writing, and she wrote many poems and stories. She and her sisters also kept journals. The journals were not secret, however, because the girls let their parents read them whenever they wanted to.

Their mother often wrote little notes in their journals, which they liked for her to do. It was a special way of talking to each other.

Louisa and her sisters did not go to school but were taught by their father. He had a way of teaching them the alphabet that always made them laugh. He used his body to make each letter. One of the girls' favorites was the letter *s,* because it required such a funny pose. Then Mr. Alcott would hiss like a goose, so they would also learn the sound of the letter *s.*

No matter how clever her father was, however, Louisa never managed to like arithmetic or grammar! Her favorite subjects were reading, writing, history, and geography.

During this time Bronson Alcott did not have a school of his own. He made some money chopping wood and working on neighbors' farms. He also grew vegetables in the garden to support his family, which had a new member—a little baby girl who was named after her mother—Abigail May, but called May. (Now there were four "little women.")

Mrs. Alcott, called "Marmee" by her

daughters, loved her husband very much, even though he failed at many things and was not able to support the family very well. She knew he was a special man who had to live his life in a certain way.

Marmee was busy all the time, cooking, cleaning, sewing, or taking care of her family in one way or another. She believed that love, being together as a family, and helping others were more important than having money. No matter how busy she was, she always had time for hugs and kisses, and for wiping away tears when there was trouble or someone was hurt. It was this feeling of warmth and love that Louisa wrote about when she grew up.

Anna, Louisa, and Elizabeth knew that they did not have much money, but they did not worry about it then. They had too much fun making up plays and acting them out in the barn, running through the woods and meadows, or having their weekly Saturday night pillow fights with their father.

Anna and Louisa also helped their mother around the house as much as they could. Anna was patient and good at housework. In fact, she was just like the oldest sister, Meg March, about whom Louisa wrote in *Little Women*. Louisa did not like housework, but she did her share.

Mrs. Alcott and her daughters cooked in the fireplace because they had no stove. The family ate mostly bread, fruit, vegetables, and cooked grain. They did not believe in eating meat.

Living in Germantown among the Quakers had taught the Alcotts the pleasures of living simply and sharing with others. A friend who came to visit them noticed they were eating only two meals a day because they were giving the third to a family who had less than they had. Even so, the house was a very jolly, noisy place, filled with laughter, love, and gentle jokes. Louisa and her family were very happy there.

Working Together

THE ALCOTTS SPENT A PLEASANT WINTER in Concord, but in the spring there were new developments. Bronson was planning to go to England. He had received a letter from some people who agreed with his ideas about education and wanted him to come and visit them. They had named a school after him and thought he would like to see it. Bronson wanted to go, but there was no money for the trip until his good friend Mr. Emerson got the money for him. In May 1842 Bronson sailed off, full of hope that this trip would lead to things that would make life better for the family.

Bronson was gone for six months. During that time Abba worked hard to take care of the family by herself. She was the one who now taught the girls and worried about how to pay all the bills. She was there alone with four children to take care of and no money coming in. They all hoped that Bronson would come back soon and that he would then have more chances for work. They loved getting his letters, which were always interesting, but they missed him very much.

When Bronson came home in October, he was not alone. He had with him three Englishmen—Charles Lane, his son William, and Henry Wright. Louisa and her sisters had not known about this beforehand. Soon they began to understand that the men would be staying with them in the small house for the winter. In the spring they would be part of a plan Bronson had for a new way of life. A bigger house would have to be found, and the family would move once more.

Abba was worried about how they would get through the winter. Their house had really been too small for six people, and now there were nine. And they didn't have any more money than they had before. What would become of them? Even her generous heart was sorely taxed at this point.

One night there was almost no wood in the shed, and Abba was very worried. All of a sudden there was a knock on the door. A kind neighbor had brought over a load of wood to help them out. Abba was very happy. But a short time later Bronson came in smiling. He felt good because he had just given away all the wood to a poor man with a sick baby who had no wood. Bronson said it was lucky that they had had some wood to give.

This time Abba got really angry. She told Bronson that he should remember that they had a baby, too, and that their house was also very cold.

Just then there was another knock on the door. A second neighbor, who did not know what the first had done, was standing there with another load of wood. Soon there was a roaring fire in the fireplace, and the house was warm and cozy again.

"I knew that God would take care of us," said Bronson.

Somehow they managed to get through the winter, and spring finally came. The men found an old, empty farmhouse twenty miles away, and in June they packed their things in a little covered wagon and drove away in the rain. They were about to begin a life that no one had ever tried before.

Bronson's plan was to have a place where people could work together in peace and love. Everyone would share the work and whatever they could grow on the land. The land would belong to everyone who lived and worked there.

Bronson and his friends believed that it was wrong to kill animals for food. They wore linen clothes, because they did not want to take covering away from sheep. And they did not use cotton because cotton was produced by slave labor, and they were against slavery. Most of all, they believed in living loving, thoughtful lives.

It would take everything they had to make their plan a success. But Bronson was certain that many other people would join them in this special new life. In the meantime, it was just the nine of them, including the five children.

Their one horse trudged bravely through the mud to the big old farmhouse that was to be their new home. Even though they were all tired and wet from the trip, they were excited to start their new adventure.

Louisa was ten now and old enough to understand that she was part of something that was special and different.

Bronson and his friends decided to name the place Fruitlands. That very name showed all the hope that was attached to their plan, because at the time only some old apple trees grew around the house. But in their minds the land would soon be blossoming with all kinds of new fruit trees that they would plant.

Everyone at Fruitlands had to work hard. Since Abba was the only grown woman, she needed all the help she could get. Louisa cleaned, ironed, and cooked. Sometimes she and Anna made a whole dinner by themselves. But there was still plenty of time for them to play and for Louisa to go running through the fields in the morning, which was something she loved to do. This is from the journal Louisa kept at Fruitlands in 1843. It tells something about what her life was like then.

September 1st—I rose at five and had my bath. I love cold water! Then we had our singing-lesson with Mr. Lane. After breakfast I washed dishes, and ran on the hill till nine, and had some thoughts,—it was so beautiful up there. . . . We had bread and fruit for dinner. I read and walked and played till supper-time. We sang in the evening. As I went to bed the moon came up very brightly and looked at me. I felt sad because I have been cross today, and did not mind Mother. I cried and then I felt better. . . .

No one is quite sure exactly when this happened, but one day when Louisa was working in the kitchen she had an experience she never forgot. She was standing near a large brick oven that had an iron door. All of a sudden she heard a strange sound coming from inside the oven. She opened the door and looked in. Looking back out at her was a thin black man who seemed very afraid. Louisa quickly slammed the door and ran to get her mother.

Abba told her that the man was a runaway slave from the South. They were helping to hide him until he could make his way to freedom in Canada. Abba told Louisa that she must keep this a secret and not say anything to anyone. If the man was found, he would be beaten and brought back in chains to his owner. It was at this moment

that Louisa saw what slavery really was, and the picture in her mind stayed with her for the rest of her life.

As the summer passed, the apples grew big on the trees at Fruitlands, and the grain was almost ready for harvesting. The men had cut and stacked the grain to dry. Then they were asked to make a trip to speak to a group about their ideas. Bronson and his friends thought the grain would be all right for a few days until they got back, so off they went, leaving Fruitlands in the hands of Abba and the children.

Things were fine the first day, but on the second day dark clouds filled the sky and Abba knew that rain was on the way. She also knew that rain would spoil the grain, which they needed to get through the winter. Quickly she called the children to her. She told them to bring bags, baskets, and anything else in which grain could be carried. She took her best linen sheets to spread on the ground. They all ran back and forth gathering the grain and dumping it on the sheets, which they then dragged to the barn. It was backbreaking work, but they did not stop. When the rain finally came, most of the grain was safely stored.

No matter how tired she was, Louisa wrote in her journal almost every evening. Usually she wrote about the day's activities or about her own troubled thoughts or efforts to control her bad temper.

In 1843 she wrote:

September 14th—. . . I ran in the wind and played be a horse, and had a lovely time in the woods with Anna and Lizzie. We were fairies, and made gowns and paper wings. I "flied" the highest of all. . . .

October 8th—When I woke up, the first thought I got was, "It's Mother's birthday: I must be very good." I ran and wished her a happy birthday and gave her my kiss. After breakfast we gave her our presents. I had a moss cross and a piece of poetry for her. . . .

October 12th—After lessons I ironed. We all went to the barn and husked corn. It was good fun. . . .

November 29th—It was Father's and my birthday. We had some nice presents. We played in the snow before school. . . . Father asked us in the eve what fault troubled us most. I said my bad temper. . . .

December—. . . Had a splendid run, and got a box of cones to burn. Sat and heard the pines sing a long time. . . . Had good dreams, and woke now and then to think, and watch the moon. I had a pleasant time with my mind, for it was happy.

Some other people had come to join the group at Fruitlands, and everyone worked very hard. In spite of all that was done, however, by the winter it was clear that things were not working out as Bronson had planned, and some men were leaving. Some left because the work was too hard, others because the life there was too cold and uncomfortable.

Bronson began to have long talks with Charles Lane about what had gone wrong. But Mr. Lane was not as discouraged. He simply felt that some changes should be made. The Shaker village was across the river from Fruitlands. Mr. Lane had gone to visit it and had been impressed with the neat fields and thriving orchards. Like Bronson and his friends at Fruitlands, the Shakers owned their property together and shared the work. But in their village members of one family did not live in the same house. Men, women, and children all lived in separate houses. Most of the children were orphans who had been given to the Shakers to raise.

When the situation did not get better at Fruitlands, Bronson and Mr. Lane went to visit the Shakers more often. Mr. Lane wanted to run Fruitlands the way the Shakers ran their village. He even wanted Bronson to send Abba, Anna, Louisa, Lizzie, and little May away and forget they were ever a family. Mr. Lane felt that Bronson's family ties interfered with their work and their grand plan. And Abba felt that he was interfering with her family life and was becoming more and more angry. At one point she even threatened to leave Fruitlands and take the children with her.

Bronson loved his family very much, but he also loved his ideas. He thought a lot about what Abba and Mr. Lane had said. Still, he could not make up his mind. The children were very afraid. They did not know what was to become of them. Finally, when Mr. Lane was away in Boston, Bronson decided to have a family meeting and ask Abba, Anna, and Louisa what he should do. Abba and the children knew that they wanted to stay together as a family. That night Louisa wrote in her journal:

In the eve father and mother and Anna and I had a long talk. I was very unhappy and we all cried. Anna and I cried in bed, and I prayed God to keep us all together.

Louisa's prayers were answered, because soon after, her father decided to keep the family together. When Mr. Lane returned from Boston, Bronson met with him, and after that Lane and his son left Fruitlands for good. The Alcotts were together as a family once again.

A Room of Her Own

Even though Bronson had decided to remain with his family and loved them very much, the failure of Fruitlands had hurt him deeply. He had worked hard to make his dream come true, and now that there was no chance of success, it seemed he did not have the will to live. He became very ill. Too weak to speak or eat, he stayed in bed day after day.

Abba remained strong during this difficult time. She took care of her husband and daughters the way she always had. Louisa and her sisters were terribly worried about their father, but their mother's steady, loving presence must have been a great comfort to them. And gradually Bronson did begin to get better.

Since it was now clear that they would not be able to run Fruitlands by themselves, it was necessary for them to find another place

31

to live. With the help of her faithful brother Samuel, Abba found a house to rent in the nearby village of Still River. It was called Brick Ends. On the day they moved, Bronson was still so weak that he had to be carried out of the house wrapped in blankets. They placed him gently on a wooden sled, since that seemed the best way to carry him over the snow to their new house.

The Alcotts lived in Still River for eight months. After that they stayed with a friend in Concord for a short time, and then they moved to Boston where both Abba and Bronson hoped to find work.

Two years after they left Fruitlands the Alcotts moved back to Concord, a town they loved for its peace and beauty, and because many of their friends lived there. Abba had inherited some money from her father, and they were able to buy their own house for the first time. Their friend Mr. Emerson also helped with money and ideas. Thirteen-year-old Louisa was excited to be living in a new place again.

They named their house Hillside. It was a big wooden house with several other buildings around it—a barn, sheds, and a wheel maker's shop.

Louisa had wanted a room of her own for a long time and had given up hope of ever having it. In a note to her mother she once wrote: "I have been thinking about my little room, which I suppose I shall never have. I should want to be there all the time, and I should go there and sing and think."

Abba wanted her daughter to have that little room, too, and when they moved to Hillside, she thought of a way to do it. She had the wheel maker's shop cut in two and had each half put on an end of the house. In one of these new wings was a little room which was to be Louisa's very own. There she could read and write, or do whatever she wanted to do.

In that room Louisa also thought about her family. She didn't want her mother and father to have to worry about money forever. And she wanted her sisters to have everything in life they desired. It was at this time that she promised herself to take care of them all—a promise she was later able to keep better than she ever thought possible.

Louisa loved her little room at Hillside, and she also loved the big barn which was on the property. It turned out to be a great place for putting on the plays that Louisa loved to write.

It wasn't long after the Alcotts moved to Hillside that Louisa wrote a three-act play. She and her sisters put on the play in the barn for many of their friends and neighbors. Louisa liked to write about beautiful princesses in trouble and princes who came to help them. She liked playing the prince so that she could speak in a loud, low voice, flash her wooden sword, and move in a quick and dashing way. Anna always played the sweet, gentle princess. Elizabeth and May took the smaller parts. But everyone had fun.

The first play they put on was such a success that Louisa worked even harder writing more plays. When she got tired, she would run out into the garden.

Louisa was also good at thinking up costumes. And she was clever at making all kinds of things out of old pieces of cloth and odds and ends. She even made a pair of boots once!

Mr. Emerson was always a good friend to all the Alcotts. One thing that was important to Louisa was that he let her use his library whenever she liked. She could choose any book she wanted to read. And sometimes he would pick out a book for her.

Mr. Emerson might have been the one who suggested that Louisa start a little school in the barn when she was sixteen, so that she could help earn money for her family. His children made up most of the students. Louisa was naturally lively and friendly, so her students liked her. And she had learned a lot from her father, which helped to make her a good teacher. But Louisa did not really like teaching, because it made her stay in one place too long. She was just as eager to get out and run as her students were. Since Louisa really wanted to help her family, however, she stuck with it.

One of the students who made teaching more enjoyable for Louisa was Ellen Emerson, Mr. Emerson's young daughter. Louisa and Ellen were very fond of each other and often visited each other's house. To amuse Ellen, Louisa began to write stories that were very different from the ones she had written before. These short stories about birds, fields, and flowers were her first stories for children, and she later called them "flower fables." After she read them to Ellen, she put them on the pile with the other plays and stories she had written. She did not share them with anyone else.

The move back to Concord was good for the Alcotts in some ways. They had their own house and were near friends they loved. However, Bronson was still not able to earn much money. In the summer Bronson's vegetable garden provided most of their food, but in the winter life would become more difficult again, and there were also debts to be paid. Abba knew that if Bronson could not find work he wanted to do, she would have to.

Finally, through a friend, Abba was offered a job in Boston as a visitor to the poor. This was part of the beginnings of social work. It was the kind of work Abba liked to do, and she was good at it. She would visit the poor and decide the best way to help them.

Abba felt that moving to Boston was the best plan for her family. Bronson was also interested because he felt he might have more opportunities there for giving talks and for meeting people. Perhaps he might even start a new school, a journal, a press, or a club. He was beginning to get new ideas again and to feel more as he had when they first moved to Boston from Pennsylvania.

Louisa did not want to move to Boston. She would rather not have given up her walks and runs in the beautiful Concord Woods and easy access to Mr. Emerson's library, not to mention the great man himself. Also, Louisa had always been happiest when she could be alone with her own thoughts, and being crowded into small city rooms would make that more difficult.

At this point, though, Louisa had no choice. The decision to move was made, and the family found someone to rent Hillside. Then they took rooms in the South End of Boston. Louisa, who was now a tall, shy six-teen-year-old, knew that life would be very different for her there.

Helping Out

SINCE LOUISA HAD EXPERIENCE TEACHING in Concord, she thought of it as a way to earn money for her family in Boston. She also sewed and took care of small children. Of her teaching, Louisa wrote:

August, 1850—School is hard work, and I feel as though I should like to run away from it. But my children get on; so I travel up every day, and do my best.

I get very little time to write or think; for my working days have begun. . . .

Members of the family mostly went their separate ways during the day. Abba went to work, Bronson gave talks about his ideas, which people paid very little money to hear, Anna and Louisa taught, May went to school, and Elizabeth stayed home and did the housework. At night the family would gather to talk about what each one had done during the day. Sometimes Abba would read to them or talk about her own childhood.

But Louisa wanted to do more. So when a man came to ask Abba if she knew of a young woman who would help out his sick sister, Louisa jumped at the chance. She was told that her work would be to read to the sister, do some light housework, and live as one of the family.

Louisa was very excited about going to work for this man. She pictured herself being helpful and being happy and loved in return. But Abba tried to talk her out of it. Louisa had never worked for anyone but friends before and did not really know this man. Louisa was sure she was doing the right thing, however. So she told the man she would come to work for him.

Louisa had asked the man what her pay would be, but he did not really answer her in a direct way. He led her to believe that she would be such a part of the family that she wouldn't need to worry about that. Louisa's sisters laughed at her and her mother still worried, but Louisa's mind was made up.

The man's sister's name was Miss Eliza.

Louisa told her that she would try the work for one month. And what a month it turned out to be! There was no such thing as reading or light housework. Louisa was made to carry heavy pails of water from the well or coal from the shed. She had to clean the house, wash the floors, and shovel snow! It was hardly the easy work the man had said it was going to be.

Louisa was very angry and unhappy, but she knew this had happened because she hadn't been careful enough. She should have taken more time to find out about the job. Still, she had agreed to stay a month and so she did. And during that whole time no one said anything about paying her.

When the month was almost over, Louisa told the man and his sister that she would be leaving. Miss Eliza cried so much that Louisa felt sorry for her and agreed to stay until someone else could be found to do the work. Louisa had a soft heart, but again she was not thinking clearly. It took three more weeks before they found someone.

When it was time for Louisa to go, the man was nowhere around. Miss Eliza cried again and gave Louisa a small pocketbook with her pay for seven weeks of hard work.

Louisa did not open the pocketbook there. She was in too much of a hurry to get away from that unhappy house.

When Louisa finally opened the pocketbook, she got a terrible surprise. Inside was only four dollars! So this was what they thought was fair pay for seven weeks of hard work! Louisa was very angry and upset. It wasn't just the money; it was knowing that people could be so unfair to someone who had worked so hard. She learned an important lesson that day. It was one that she never forgot.

Louisa learned another important lesson soon after one of her father's trips. He had gone on a long journey to the West to give talks about his ideas. The Alcotts had great hopes that people would be so excited about what Bronson had to say, they would pay him very well. But when Bronson finally came home, only little May was brave enough to ask, "Well, did people pay you?"

Bronson had learned much on his trip and people had been very interested in what he

had to say, but what he pulled from his pocket was a single dollar bill. It didn't matter to him. He was happy with what he had done. "Another year, I shall do better," he said.

Everyone in the family was very quiet. Then Abba threw her arms around his neck and said, "I call that doing very well!" Louisa learned that night what real love can do. No matter what her mother's hopes were, her love for her husband was stronger than anything else. Love was what was really important in her life, and Louisa never forgot that.

Then something very exciting happened to Louisa. Her father had found one of the "flower fables" she had written for Ellen Emerson. He showed it to a friend in publishing who read it and liked it. He had it printed and paid Louisa five dollars. Louisa didn't think much of the story herself. She preferred her action stories. But she must have been very pleased to have earned money from something she had written.

People liked Louisa's story, and so the publisher asked to see the others. They were put together and published in a small book called *Flower Fables* in 1855, when Louisa was twenty-two years old. Louisa was paid thirty-two dollars for it.

In June of 1855 Louisa's cousin Lizzie invited her to spend the summer in Walpole, New Hampshire. In July the rest of the Alcotts went to stay in a friend's house nearby. Louisa loved being able to run through the fields again. She wrote more flower stories and began to think of what else she could write and sell in order to help her family.

Living and working in Boston had been very difficult for Louisa's mother, and it hadn't really solved the family's money problems, either. Abba thought that staying in Walpole would be best for her children, and so she decided to remain for the winter.

For weeks Louisa looked for any kind of work she could get, but there seemed to be nothing at all she could do in Walpole.

Anna, who was also job hunting, finally found a teaching position in an asylum in New York State and left Walpole in October.

Louisa became more and more restless

and concerned about finding work now that Anna was gone. Finally she made a very important decision. As much as she disliked leaving her family, she decided to go to Boston and see if she could do better there.

In November, the month of her twenty-third birthday, she boarded a stagecoach for Boston. She wrote in her journal:

Decided to seek my fortune; so with my little trunk of home-made clothes, $20 earned by stories sent to the "Gazette," and my MSS., I set forth with Mother's blessing one rainy day in the dullest month of the year.

As the stagecoach carried her through the cold rain, Louisa was filled with fear and hope. She especially wanted to sell a new book she had written called *Christmas Elves.* Her sister May, now a promising artist, had drawn pictures for it. One thing Louisa knew for certain was that she would not give up until she reached her goal.

Changes in the Wind

L OUISA WAS NOT ABLE TO SELL HER BOOK *Christmas Elves* in Boston. She wrote in her journal:

Found it too late to do anything with the book, so put it away and tried for teaching, sewing, or any honest work. Won't go home to sit idle while I have a head and pair of hands.

That winter Louisa lived with her cousins and earned what money she could by teaching and sewing. She also worked on her stories any time she had a chance, and she did begin to sell them for five, six, or ten dollars. Most of the stories she was writing then had very little to do with her own life or people she might have known. The subject matter of the stories was rather strange, but they were usually filled with action and drama, which many people liked.

Louisa's father wanted to help her out. He

took one of her stories to a friend of his who worked for a well-known magazine.

"Tell Louisa to stick to her teaching," the man said. "She is never going to be a writer."

But Louisa did not let that get her down. "I will *not* stick to my teaching," she said. "I *will* be a writer. And I will write for his magazine, too." And she did, though it was several years later.

It was very hard for Louisa to live alone in Boston. She missed her large, loving family. But she was quite brave and could laugh when her feelings got hurt. Also, she had always been able to pick herself up and try again when things did not go well for her.

And these *were* hard times for Louisa. News came from Walpole that May and Elizabeth were very sick with scarlet fever. They had caught it from some poor children Abba had taken care of. Louisa was needed at home, and of course she went right away. Everyone was most worried about Elizabeth. May got better, but Beth did not seem to get much stronger.

In the fall Louisa sadly went back to Boston, hoping that Beth would get well. She was able to get a little attic room in a board-inghouse. She called this room her "sky-parlor," which she wrote about as Jo's garret in *Little Women*. In April 1855 she wrote in her journal:

I am in the garret with my papers round me, and a pile of apples to eat while I write my journal, plan stories, and enjoy the patter of rain on the roof, in peace and quiet.

In order to have this room, she had to sew a certain number of hours every day for the owner of the boardinghouse. In that same April journal entry, she also wrote:

... began another tale, but found little time to work on it, with school, sewing, and housework. My winter's earnings are,

School, one quarter $50
Sewing $50
Stories $50
if I am ever paid.

In June Louisa returned to Walpole because Beth was getting weaker and weaker. Soon after she got there, the Alcotts decided to move back to Concord. They hoped they could recapture their happy days among friends at Hillside. Maybe there, Beth would get better.

They found an old house and some land not far from town. The house was in such bad shape that the owner thought the Alcotts would just tear it down. But he did not know this hardworking family! Louisa cleaned everything from top to bottom. She found places for clothes and dishes and of course—books! Together with Anna and May she painted and papered. Bronson worked hard taking care of the fruit trees and the garden. They wanted Beth to have a nice, pretty place where she could be comfortable. Because of the fruit trees, they named their new home Orchard House.

It took the Alcotts a long time to finish the house because they did everything themselves. All through the winter they worked. Meanwhile, they had to live in part of a rented house near the Concord Town Hall.

But no matter what they did or how hard they wished, Beth did not get any better. She seemed to be slowly drifting from them. Their hearts were breaking to see her so, but they knew that nothing more could be done for her. And she herself seemed to know it, too. She passed the time bravely—singing quietly, sewing, reading, or looking at the fire. She liked to have Louisa sit with her because she said it made her feel strong. On March 14, 1858, the end came quietly to Elizabeth—as quietly as she had lived. Louisa wrote:

A curious thing happened, and I will tell it here, for Dr. G. said it was a fact. A few moments after the last breath came, as Mother and I sat silently watching the shadow fall on the dear little face, I saw a light mist rise from the body, and float up and vanish in the air. Mother's eyes followed mine, and when I said, "What did you see?" she described the same light mist. Dr. G. said it was the life departing visibly.

When Beth died, the Alcotts knew that part of their hearts went with her. But Beth's quiet bravery was never to be forgotten, as readers of *Little Women* know. Louisa kept her dear sister's memory alive with her writing. In April Louisa wrote in her journal:

I don't miss her as I expected to do, for she seems nearer and dearer than before; and I am

glad to know she is safe from pain and age in some world where her innocent soul must be happy.

Death never seemed terrible to me, and now is beautiful; so I cannot fear it, but find it friendly and wonderful.

Life went on for the Alcotts in spite of this sadness. Anna went to visit some friends named the Pratts in the country. She must have had a very good time, because when she came home in April, she announced she was engaged to John Pratt.

Louisa had mixed feelings about this news. She was happy for Anna, but she was sad because she felt she was losing another sister.

In June the Alcotts finally finished fixing the house they had bought, and they moved there in July. Louisa wrote in her journal:

Went into the new house and began to settle. Father is happy; Mother glad to be at rest; Anna is in bliss with her gentle John; and May busy over her pictures. I have plans simmering, but must sweep and dust and wash my dish-pans a while longer till I see my way.

This was a difficult time for Louisa. She longed for a change. For a while it looked as though she was going to get a chance to act in a play, something that seemed very exciting to her. But that fell through. Finally she decided to return to Boston to look for work.

She had once been a teacher in the home of a little girl named Alice L., who was too sick to go out to school. There was a chance that she could be little Alice's teacher again, but nothing was certain.

Finally, through friends, Louisa was offered a job at a girls' reform school. She would have to sew for ten hours a day. Louisa wasn't afraid of hard work, but sewing from morning until night would not leave any time for writing. This bothered her very much. Still, it was the only offer she had, so she agreed to go. She packed her bag, all the while hating the thought of what she was about to do.

Just as Louisa was about to leave for the reform school, she heard from Alice's mother that she could return as Alice's teacher. Louisa wrote in her journal:

That eve, when my bag was packed and all was ready . . . came a note from Mrs. L. offering the old salary and the old place. I sang for joy . . .

Now she would be able to stay in Boston, live in her little "sky-parlor," and write. Louisa was very excited and happy. She was also proud of herself because she felt she had just passed a test of character and courage.

After her twenty-sixth birthday in November 1858, Louisa wrote:

. . . A quiet day, with many thoughts and memories.

The past year has brought us the first death and betrothal, —two events that change my life. I can see that these experiences have taken a deep hold, and changed or developed me. . . .

After my fit of despair I seem to be braver and more cheerful, and grub away with a good heart. Hope it will last, for I need all the courage and comfort I can get.

Anna and John Pratt's wedding was on May 23, 1860. Of course Louisa went home so that she could be part of it all, even though she still felt bad that Anna would be leaving home. All the Alcotts' friends came to the wedding and had a good time dancing on the grass afterward. Everyone was very happy for Anna and John.

No one knows how Louisa really felt about a wedding for herself. She liked to be free, and it seemed that she never found anyone who could be that special person for her. She also worried that she would tire of someone, the way she tired of so many things. In any case, she never married. Her heart seemed to belong to her family.

Family life for the Alcotts was quite different now. Anna was married, and May was away at art school, so Louisa stayed at home to help her mother with the housework. She worked at her writing and sold more of her stories. She was especially happy because many of them were being published by the magazine whose editor had told her to "stick to her teaching."

Even though many editors wanted her stories and were willing to pay money for them, Louisa did not think they were very good. She wrote because she wanted to earn money. It was also a way for her to escape from her difficult life into a fantasy world.

Losing Beth had changed Louisa quite a bit, however, and she was beginning to think that she could write something more meaningful. She wrote in her journal:

I feel as if I could write better now,—more truly of things I have felt and therefore *know*. I hope I shall yet do my great book, for that seems to be my work, and I am growing up to it.

She began a book she called *Moods*. It was the longest story she had ever written. In August she wrote in her journal: ". . . for four weeks I wrote all day and planned nearly all night. . . ." After that she put it away for a while and went back to writing her magazine stories. They were what paid her the most. In September Louisa wrote in her journal that she had received seventy-five dollars for a story called "Cinderella":

. . . and feel very rich. Emerson praised it, and people wrote to me about it and patted me on the head. Paid bills, and began to simmer another.

But Louisa could not always write when she wanted to. If her mother was sick, or if anyone else in the family needed her, she would quickly take over as nurse or house-keeper and put her writing aside. When Abba went to visit her brother Sam in October, Louisa took over as housekeeper again and, as she wrote humorously, "Gave my mind to it so energetically that I dreamed dip-toast, talked apple-sauce, thought pies, and wept drop-cakes."

December must have been a rather sad time for Louisa. She wrote in her journal: "A quiet Christmas; no presents but apples and flowers. No merry-making for Nan and May were gone, and Betty under the snow. But we are used to hard times. . . ."

One good thing was that Bronson was doing better with his talks, and he was also put in charge of all the schools in Concord. He finally had a chance to see his good ideas about teaching put to use.

April of 1861 brought important news to the sleepy town of Concord. Because of the attack on Fort Sumter, the Civil War began. People were surprised, even though there had been talk of war for years. No one could really believe that the conflict over slavery had actually come to this.

Louisa recorded the event in her journal.

April.—War declared with the South, and our Concord company went to Washington. A busy time getting them ready, and a sad day seeing them off; for in a little town like this we all seem like one family in times like these. At the station the scene was very dramatic, as the brave boys went away perhaps never to come back again.

I've often longed to be a man; but as I can't fight, I will content myself with working for those who can.

By working, Louisa meant sewing, for that was all women could do at the beginning of the war.

May.—Spent our May-day working for our men,—three hundred women all sewing together at the hall for two days.

When the Civil War broke out, both the North and the South believed that they would win and win quickly. It wasn't until months had passed that both sides knew it would be much harder than they first thought.

Other entries in Louisa's journal show that life went on even as the war continued.

May.—Nan found that I was wearing all the old clothes she and May left; so the two dear souls clubbed together and got me some new ones; and the great parcel, with a loving letter, came to me as a beautiful surprise.

October.—All together on Marmee's birthday. Sewing and knitting for "our boys" all the time. It seems as if a few energetic women could carry on the war better than the men do it so far.

November and December.—Wrote, read, sewed, and wanted something to do.

That "something to do" came in the form of a suggestion from Elizabeth Peabody, for whom Beth had been named. Miss Peabody was starting several kindergartens in Boston and asked Louisa if she would be in charge of one of them. Louisa wrote in her journal: *January, 1862.*—". . . Don't like to teach, but take what comes. . . ."

Louisa worked all through the winter, but she was glad when the school year ended, and she never worked as a teacher again. She was beginning to make more money with her writing and liked it much better.

Nurse Louisa

MEANWHILE, THE CIVIL WAR WENT ON and on, and before long a year had passed. Men on both sides were fighting hard and were dying. No one was winning yet. Hundreds of wounded men were coming to the hospitals, and nurses were needed to help take care of them.

Ever since the beginning of the war, Louisa had wished she could do more for the brave men who were fighting against slavery. Her father had been one of the first people to oppose slavery, and she remembered well the boy who had saved her from the Frog Pond, and the runaway slave her mother had hidden in the oven. Now she thought more and more about becoming a nurse and helping the war effort in that way. She had nursed Beth, her mother, and Cousin Lizzie, and everyone said she was very good at it. She was young, strong, and kind—just the type of person who could be very useful as a nurse.

So in November of 1862, at the age of thirty, Louisa sent a letter to someone in Washington offering to be a nurse in one of the hospitals there. Soon after, she made an entry in her journal:

December.—On the 11th I received a note from Miss H. M. Stevenson telling me to start for Georgetown next day to fill a place in the Union Hotel Hospital . . . though a hard place, help was needed.

Louisa began to pack her things and get ready to make the trip to Washington. She was very excited to be going, but off and on she wondered if she would ever come back. She would be facing lots of very hard work, sadness, and great danger from all kinds of sicknesses which she could catch from the soldiers. But Louisa felt ready to handle whatever life had in store for her.

"We had all been full of courage till the last moment came," Louisa wrote of her family, "then we all broke down. I said,

'Shall I stay, Mother?' as I hugged her close." And her mother had answered, "No, go! and the Lord be with you!" Then she smiled bravely and stood on the doorstep waving her wet handkerchief until Louisa turned the corner.

It was not easy to get from Boston to Washington in those days. Louisa had to take a train to New London, Connecticut, a boat to New York, and then another train to Washington. After that she had a long cab ride over bumpy roads to Georgetown, where the hospital was. Louisa was very tired when she finally arrived.

The hospital building had once been a big hotel, but it had not been fixed up or cleaned for many years. Louisa was given a very small room that she would be sharing with two other nurses. The room was not very pleasant at all. Many of the windows were broken and had no curtains on them. The fireplace was narrow and not much help in warming the cold room. The closet was full of bugs, and Louisa could hear rats running in the walls. As if that weren't bad enough, Louisa was warned not to leave her good things lying around because other workers might take them.

The head nurse did not waste any time putting Louisa to work. Another nurse had become sick, and Louisa was to take her place. So right away, without any training, Louisa was put in charge of a ward that had forty beds in it. She looked at the rows of old beds and knew that this was not going to be an easy job. But she was glad she had decided to come and help anyway. The first three days the hospital was not crowded, and Louisa was able to get to know her fellow workers and the sick and wounded men who were in her care.

Then things began to change quickly. A battle was lost by the North, and cries of "The wounded are coming!" rang through the halls of the hospital. Soon the rooms were filled with men who were hurt and sick. They had fought in the rain for three days and were cold and tired, as well as very dirty. Some of the men could walk and were able to stand and warm themselves around the stoves. Others were put to bed or onto stretchers on the floor.

Louisa was now put in charge of a larger ward. This one was for the men who had been hurt the most. There was so much to be done that Louisa did not know what to do first, so she asked another nurse who had been there longer.

"Wash them" was all the nurse said as she hurried on. So Louisa picked up a large tin bowl of water, a towel, and some soap, and began to gently wash the man in the bed nearest her. At first she was afraid that she would hurt him, but the happy thanks he gave her made her feel that everything would be all right.

Louisa was always on the go, taking care of the men who called out to her and the men who were not strong enough to call or even to move. It was likely that Louisa was more tired than she had ever been, but she kept going.

Louisa had the gift of being able to make people laugh. It was no wonder that the men grew to love her as she moved from bed to bed, bringing food and water, changing bandages, or just talking and laughing. Her ward became a happy place—as happy as a place like that could be, anyway.

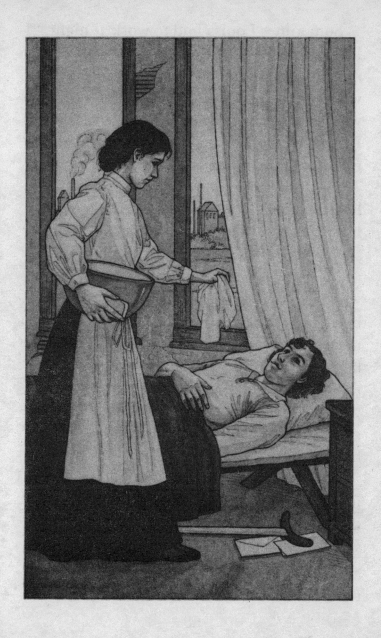

Sometimes Louisa had to work at night. "I like it," she wrote, "as it leaves me time for a morning run, which is what I need to keep well; for bad air, food, and water, work and watching, are getting to be too much for me. I trot up and down the streets in all directions. . . ."

The first time she worked at night she heard someone crying quietly. This did not happen very often, and she quickly went to see what was the matter. In the last bed in the ward was a young boy named Billy. He was only twelve years old, and his job had been to play the drum as the soldiers marched. When Louisa got to his bed, he began to cry openly. He said, "I dreamed that Kit was here and when I waked up he wasn't." He cried and cried and Louisa comforted him. Then she listened as he told his sad story.

Billy had marched along with the soldiers for miles and miles, playing his drum. He kept up with them through the rain, the snow, and the hot sun, even though he was still a young boy and was not as strong as a grown man. Finally he became sick and had to stay in his tent. He could hear the sound of the guns and his friends fighting outside. He worried about all of his friends, but he worried about Kit the most. Kit was a special friend who had always looked out for him like a big brother.

Then the sounds changed and Billy heard hundreds of feet dashing past the tent. His friends were losing this fight. Kit hurried into the tent, picked Billy up, and carried him away with the others. Even though Kit was badly hurt, he would not let anyone else carry Billy. Finally Billy fell asleep. When he woke up, he was being carried into the hospital, but Kit was not there. Another soldier told him as gently as he could that Kit had died.

Billy tried to be brave, but when he dreamed about laughing with Kit around the campfire, everything came back to him again and he began to cry. Louisa stayed with him until he felt better and was able to fall asleep again.

After Billy had fallen asleep, Louisa heard a sound behind her. It was a wounded man who was walking in his sleep and saying,

"I'm going home." Louisa tried to wake him up, but it was no use, and she was not able to stop him from walking around. Louisa was very worried that he would hurt himself. Finally another wounded man got out of bed and helped her. He was big and strong and was able to lead the sleepwalker back to his bed, and the room became quiet once more.

One of the men Louisa took care of was a blacksmith named John. He was very strong and was so tall that he had to have a bed that was longer than the others. Everyone talked of how John had insisted that his friends be taken care of before himself. But John was very badly hurt. The doctor told Louisa that John was going to die, and he wanted Louisa to tell him. This must have been very hard for Louisa, but she did it.

John took the news calmly. His only request was that he wanted to write letters to his mother and younger brother and sisters. He told Louisa what he wanted to say in the letters, and she wrote everything down for him. Before the war he had been taking care of the whole family, and now his younger brother would have to carry on. "I hope the answer will come in time for me to see it," was all he said.

The night he died, he called for Louisa and she stood by while his best friend said good-bye to him. When it was all over, she also felt that she had lost a dear friend.

Louisa came to know many brave men in the hospital. And she wanted her loved ones to know them, too. So whatever free time she had she used to write letters home about these men.

As the days went by, Billy got well and went home, and so did many others. They all said good-bye to Louisa and gave her their thanks. But while Louisa was helping others, she began to feel unwell herself. She got what seemed to be a cold, but she didn't get better. What she had was a very bad sickness called typhoid. It came on slowly. Louisa became thin and pale. It was difficult for her to move around and do her work. The doctors saw how sick she was and told her to stay in her room and rest. Louisa wanted to keep helping, but she was too sick to work, so she stayed in her room and sewed and wrote letters. She never told anyone at home how sick she was. Finally she got so weak that a doctor told her that she would have to go home, but she refused to go.

A week passed and she hardly knew what was going on around her. She could not eat. All she wanted was water. Finally someone sent for Louisa's father, and he came for her. She still did not want to go, so he stayed and took care of her for five days.

Then it became clear even to Louisa that she was too sick herself to be able to help others, so she agreed to leave. Bronson packed her things, and lots of people came to see her off. Many gave her small gifts. Even though Louisa had been at the hospital only a little more than a month, she had made many friends and would be missed.

It was a long trip home, but Louisa only remembered seeing May's face at the station and her mother's worried face at home. She also remembered getting into bed, believing "that the house was roofless, and no one wanted to see me." It seems likely, however, that Louisa's father remembered the difficult trip with his very sick daughter for as long as he lived.

"A Girls' Book"

LOUISA WAS SICK FOR WEEKS AND WEEKS. She stayed in bed and did not really know what was going on around her. When she came home it was winter. By the time she started to feel better, it was getting to be spring. In 1863 she wrote:

February.—Found a queer, thin, big-eyed face when I looked in the glass; did n't know myself at all; and when I tried to walk discovered that I could n't, and cried because my legs would n't go.

Never having been sick before, it was all new and very interesting when I got quiet enough to understand matters.

March.—Began to get about a little, sitting up nearly all day, eating more regularly, and falling back into my old ways. . . . I cleared out my piece-bags and dusted my books, feeling as tired as if I had cleaned the whole house.

Abba had been very worried about Louisa during this time. And Bronson seemed all tired out from taking care of her. The family needed something happy to happen, and it did! Anna was expecting her first child, and on a cold wet day in March, Bronson arrived from Boston, "snowy and beaming," with the words, "Good news! Good news! Anna has a fine boy."

". . . we opened our mouths and screamed for about two minutes," Louisa wrote in a letter to Anna. "Then Mother began to cry; I began to laugh; and May to pour out questions; while Papa beamed upon us all—red, damp, and shiny, the picture of a proud old Grandpa. . . .

"May and I at once taxed our brains for a name, and decided upon 'Amos Minot Bridge Bronson May Sewall Alcott Pratt'. . . ." Louisa and May thought the name would make every member of both large families happy. But the new parents decided on Frederic Alcott Pratt, which seemed much better for a little baby!

When Louisa was on night duty at the hospital, she had made up a poem for her teacher and friend Henry David Thoreau. He had died the year before, on May 6, 1862, and she missed him very much. Louisa's sickness had made her forget the poem for a while, but as she got better, she remembered it, wrote it down, and kept it with her other papers. Her father came across the poem one day. He read it to friends who sent it to a well-known magazine, where it was printed, praised, and paid for. "Had a fresh feather in my cap," wrote Louisa, ". . . and . . . I liked the $10 nearly as well as the honor of being 'a new star'. . . ."

Louisa's writing was again being noticed by others. An editor of a paper had a chance to see some of Louisa's letters to her family from the hospital. He thought they were so interesting that he named them "Hospital Sketches" and printed them in the paper. Soon a great many people learned about Billy, John, and the others Louisa had met. At that time people were very worried about their own fathers, brothers, and sons in the war, so they were eager to read how things were for men who got hurt and had to go to a hospital.

This writing was not like Louisa's adventure writing, because it was real. These things had actually happened to Louisa, and that made her writing very clear and true. When she wrote about brave men who could still laugh even though they were badly hurt, people understood and were interested. They wanted her to write more, so when she got stronger, she did. Then "Hospital Sketches" were printed in a book, and an even greater number of people read them. Louisa wrote:

If there was ever an astonished young woman, it is myself, for things have gone so swimmingly of late I don't know who I am. A year ago I had no publisher, and went begging with my wares; now *three* have asked me for something, several papers are ready to print my contributions. . . . There is a sudden hoist for a meek and lowly scribbler, who was told to "stick to her teaching.". . . .

The "Sketches" never earned much money for Louisa, but it showed her the "style" that would be successful for her— writing from her own life's experience.

Louisa was becoming well known, so her publishers wanted another book from her. She showed them *Moods,* but they said it was too long. After she fixed it so they liked it, *Moods* was printed in 1864.

Louisa had hoped to return to nursing after she got better. But as the months went by, it became clear to her that she was no longer strong enough to do that kind of work. The war finally ended after four years, and Louisa spent most of her time on her writing. She still could not work very long hours, but for the first time she was earning enough from her writing to really help her family. And another happy thing was that Anna had given birth to a second boy, John Pratt, Jr., in 1865.

Meanwhile, a man named Mr. Thomas Niles, who was in charge of the publishing company of Roberts Brothers, had been reading Louisa's writing. In 1867 he had a very special idea. He thought Louisa should write "a girls' book." At first Louisa did not like the idea. She told her mother she didn't know anything about girls, except for the girls in her own family. Even so, she started to work on the book in May of 1868. And once she started, it didn't seem so hard after all. She wrote about things that had really happened to her and to her sisters as they were growing up, both the good times and bad. And she wrote about what was important to them all—love, reading, and each other. Louisa decided to call the book *Little Women*, and it was about the March family.

Mr. Niles was eager to see what Louisa was writing, so when she had finished a few chapters, she mailed them to him. Mr. Niles read the chapters carefully, but they were not what he had expected. He wrote to Louisa saying he was not sure people would be interested in her book. This did not worry Louisa. She now felt that *Little Women* would be welcomed by young readers, because it told what life was actually like for little girls in those days. At the time there were no such books.

When Louisa finished *Little Women*, Mr. Niles read it but still was not sure he wanted to publish it. However, he was a smart man, and he did not want to turn it down without being sure. He had a wonderful idea. He asked some young girls to read the book and tell him what *they* thought about it.

The girls were delighted with it. The book was not like anything they had ever read before, because it was so true to the way they lived themselves. And the writer seemed to understand them *very* well.

It was no wonder that *Little Women* seemed real to those girls. The events in the book had really happened to Louisa and her sisters. The March family was like the Alcott family. Marmee was really like Louisa's mother, Meg was like Anna, Beth was like Elizabeth, Amy was like May, and Jo was like Louisa herself. All the highs and lows, ups and downs, plays and pillow fights had actually happened.

So Mr. Niles decided to publish *Little Women,* and the book was a big hit. Louisa was very happy because she knew she had finally done her best work. People all around the world were excited about what she had written. The book sold well, and Louisa became rich.

After a lifetime of being poor, she now had money to spend. She made Orchard

House warm and comfortable, at last, and she gave her mother, father, and sisters whatever they needed or wanted. It was what she had always hoped she could do. There was nothing Louisa wanted for herself but that. Her own room at Orchard House, now a museum, is the same today as it was then—small and plain, with not much in it.

Because *Little Women* became such a favorite book, Mr. Niles thought Louisa should write another about the same people. The first book was published in October 1868. Louisa began work on the second in November and sent it to him on New Year's Day. People liked it as well as the first. Both books together make up what we know as the whole book of *Little Women* today. Mr. Niles's company never had a bigger success.

Mr. Niles asked Louisa to write another book. Louisa agreed to do it, but this time she wrote about a girl named Polly and the hard time she had making a living. It was rather like what had happened to Louisa when she was younger. She called the book *An Old-Fashioned Girl.*

When Louisa got the sad news that

Anna's husband, John, had died, leaving Anna with two small sons and very little money, Louisa wrote another book called *Little Men*. She wanted all the money from the book to go to Anna and the children. *Little Men* sold thousands of copies on the very first day it came out, and Anna and her sons were well taken care of.

Louisa thought about her family all the time, and now her greatest worry was her mother, who seemed to be getting weaker and weaker. Louisa stayed in Concord much more now, so that she could be near her.

Little Men was almost as popular as *Little Women,* so Louisa went on to write other greatly loved books. *Eight Cousins* and *Rose in Bloom* were among them. Thanks to her successful books, she was able to afford to take care of Anna and her sons, send her sister May to Europe to study art, and give her mother and father every possible comfort. Louisa's heart was also full because she knew she was loved, not only by her family, but by thousands of people she had never even met who had read and loved the books she had written.

A Job Well Done

THINGS WERE GOING WELL FOR ALL THE Alcotts now. Even Bronson's talks in the West were interesting more people. He thought it was all because of Louisa, but that really was not true. People were finally starting to understand his ideas, which had been so far ahead of their time.

Whenever Bronson got ready for a trip, Louisa packed his bag. Now that she had money, Louisa made sure her father had everything he needed—new shirts, warm socks, and even a new coat. Louisa also helped to buy Henry Thoreau's house for Anna and the boys to live in. It was more comfortable and closer to town than their other house.

Meanwhile, Abba Alcott was getting weaker with every passing day. She was happy and not in any pain, but she was dying even so, and it was her wish to move to

Anna's house with Louisa. Bronson had returned from his latest trip to the West, so he was with Abba when she closed her eyes for the last time.

Abba had been so important to all of them, and the house would seem very strange without her. "Father goes about, being restless with his anchor gone," wrote Louisa. Once, when she was writing about what was and what was not taken from life in *Little Women*, Louisa said, "Mrs. March is all true, only not half good enough." This shows how much Louisa loved her mother. She must have missed her terribly. Soon after her mother's death she wrote: "My duty is done, and now I shall be glad to follow her." When Bronson went away on another trip, there was only Anna and Louisa to comfort each other in their loss. "She was so loyal, tender, and true;" wrote Louisa, "life was hard for her, and no one understood all she had to bear but we, her children."

May had not come home for her mother's funeral. Louisa thought it best that she stay in Europe, where she had "tender friends" to take care of her during this sad time. However, it wasn't long before Louisa got the happy news that May was going to be the wife of one of these "tender friends," whose name was Ernest Nieriker. May was married March 22, 1878.

Louisa wanted very much to go and visit May and her new husband, but she couldn't because of her poor health. She had never regained her strength after her bout with typhoid. Medical knowledge was not as advanced as it is today, and when Louisa was sick with typhoid, she had been given large amounts of calomel. The calomel cured the typhoid, but calomel contains a great deal of mercury, which stays in the body and poisons it very slowly. Louisa complained about headaches, dizziness, and not being able to sleep, but no one knew what was wrong with her at the time. So as much as she wanted to go to Europe, she was forced to stay home.

A year later there was more happy news. May had given birth to a little girl she had named Louisa May. The older Louisa May was beside herself with joy. May's only wish now was that she could see her sister. Louisa didn't know why, but she began to worry about May. And it turned out that she was right to worry. About a month later Mr. Emerson came to see her. He had a paper in his hand and tears were in his eyes.

"My child, I wish I could prepare you, but—alas—alas—" he said. All he could do was hand her the paper, which was a telegram from May's husband. He wanted Mr. Emerson to give Louisa the bad news.

"I *am* prepared," said Louisa. "I *felt* the truth before the news came," she later wrote. Louisa tried to be strong as she read the terrible words that told her that May was dead. She learned later, from letters, that May had died on December 29, 1879, after three weeks of fever, "Happy and painless most of the time."

May had thought of her good sister Louisa as she was dying and wanted to give her the things dearest to her heart. "She wished me to have her baby and her pictures," Louisa wrote. "Rich payment for the little I could do for her." Louisa could not believe that her gay, carefree younger sister was dead. She had always made life so bright for them all. Louisa did not know if she could bear the sadness. She and her father wrote poems about May and that helped to make them feel better. They also planned for the arrival of the baby, who was known as Lulu.

Louisa was not well enough to go to Europe to get Lulu. Instead, she sent a trusted nurse. And on September 18, 1880, Lulu arrived in Boston, carried in the arms of the ship's captain himself. Louisa was so happy to see this dear child who looked so much like May. It was hard for her to believe that Lulu would now be her own little girl. That night Louisa went into Lulu's room many times to see her sleeping in her tiny bed. Was she really there? Louisa asked herself.

Taking care of Lulu helped Louisa get over her grief. She bought a summer cottage by the sea, where they could be together, and she made up songs and stories to make Lulu happy. Lulu soon became a big part of Louisa's life.

During this time, Louisa also worked on her book *Jo's Boys,* which had been promised to her fans. In her journal entry of July 1886, she wrote about finishing *Jo's Boys* and said,

". . . the children will be happy, and my promise kept."

In March of 1888 Louisa went to visit her father, who was very sick and living apart from her. She thought it would be the last time she would see him, and she was right, for he died on March fourth. While driving home, Louisa caught cold, became very ill the next day, and died on March sixth, just two days after her father. Soon after, Lulu was sent back to Europe to live with her father's family.

But death can never really touch people like Louisa May Alcott, for she lives on in the wonderful stories that she has left behind. For over one hundred years young readers have been delighted with the warmth and truth of her writing. And she will live in the hearts of all who have read and enjoyed her books.

Highlights in the Life of
LOUISA MAY ALCOTT

1832 Louisa May Alcott is born November 29 in Germantown, Pennsylvania.

1835 Elizabeth Sewall Alcott is born June 24 in Boston, Massachusetts.

1840 Abba May Alcott is born July 26 in Concord, Massachusetts.

1845 Louisa begins to write plays.

1848 Louisa opens her school in the barn and writes the stories published later as *Flower Fables*.

1852 Louisa's first story is printed.

1855 Louisa's first book, *Flower Fables*, is published.

1858 Elizabeth dies March 14.

1860 Anna marries John Bridge Pratt May 23.

1862 Louisa teaches in a kindergarten, volunteers as a nurse in November, and goes to Georgetown Hospital in December.

1863 Louisa gets sick and is taken home in January. In March Anna's son Frederic Alcott Pratt is born.

1865 Anna's second son, John Sewall Pratt, is born June 24 (Elizabeth's birthday).

1868 Louisa begins *Little Women* in May. It is published in October.

1869 The second part of *Little Women* is published in May.

1871 John Pratt dies.

1877 Abba Alcott dies November 25.

1878 May marries Ernest Nieriker March 22.

1879 Louisa May Nieriker is born November 8. May dies December 29.

1880 Lulu Nieriker arrives in Boston to live with Louisa.

1888 Bronson Alcott dies March 4. Louisa May Alcott dies March 6.

Works by Louisa May Alcott

Novels for Children:

1868–69	*Little Women*
1870	*An Old-Fashioned Girl*
1871	*Little Men*
1875	*Eight Cousins*
1876	*Rose in Bloom*
1878	*Under the Lilacs*
1880	*Jack and Jill*
1886	*Jo's Boys*
1888	*A Garland for Girls*

Collections:

1854	*Flower Fables*
1872–82	*Aunt Jo's Scrapbag* (6 volumes)
1872	*My Boys*
1872	*Shawl-Straps*
1874	*Cupid and Chow-Chow*
1876	*Silver Pitchers*
1878	*My Girls*
1879	*Jimmy's Cruise in the Pinafore*
1882	*An Old-Fashioned Thanksgiving*
1882	*Proverb Stories*
1884	*Spinning-Wheel Stories*
1886–89	*Lulu's Library* (3 volumes)

For Adults

1863	*Hospital Sketches*
1864	*Moods*
1873	*Work*
1877	*Modern Mephistopheles*